The Shack

in the

Woods

BY AMANDA BLACKWOOD

MANDOLIN PUBLISHING

Published by the Mandolin Publishing Group
For more information, Find us on Facebook
https://www.facebook.com/Mandolinpublishing

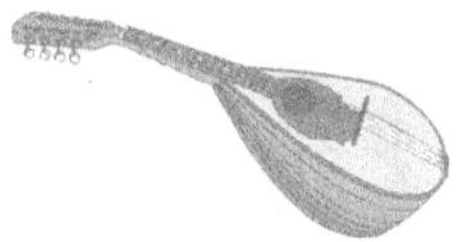

DEDICATED TO DAN

I should have been a better role model. I'm sorry I wasn't. But I'll never regret the adventures we had.

THE SHACK

In The

WOODS

Part One

THE SHACK

In The

WOODS

I guess looking back on my youth I'm starting to understand just how reckless I was. At the time I couldn't understand why my parents were constantly in a panic about the things I would do. I have to admit that even though I was a relatively good kid by my own standards, my parents themselves had completely different standards entirely. When I didn't live up to them, then it was instantly assumed that I was doing far worse than what I was actually guilty of. I didn't have the greatest of influences around me and I did enjoy my time with some of the worst influences I could find.

My friend Jimmy taught me of the joys involved with skipping school on occasion in order to go bowling, or just driving around town with friends and flipping a coin at intersections in order to decide which way we would turn. Living in Utah there weren't a lot of other things to do in the late 1990s other than drugs, and that wasn't a road I was willing to travel even in my reckless days. Instead, the flip of a coin eventually had us exploring Antelope Island one day. Jimmy identified as a "Goth" which meant he wore head to toe black clothing and black lipstick, so he clearly seemed like a much worse influence than he was in my life. We were just a couple of broken people looking for something to feel in the world other than desperation and pain.

Another friend of mine taught me the value of lying to my parents about her mother being home during a sleepover. She was a very dear friend of mine at the time and we had always been close. One night when spending some time at her house for a sleepover, there was an unfortunate accident that left me with a gaping wound on the back of my arm. Her mother had gone out that night to be with friends in a bar, and when I needed to be rushed to the hospital at nearly 11 o'clock at night, my father was much less than pleased with our decision to not tell them that an adult wouldn't be home that night. In all fairness, I didn't know about that decision until after I'd arrived at my friend's house. Seven stitches and very much pain later, I was forbidden to ever go to her house again, and I was grounded for an extraordinary amount of time.

Other friends of mine were very much into the drug scene I was dead set against getting involved in, but my young mind was still quite curious about it all. I was constantly invited to the parties they would have at their homes, and though I rarely ever went, I never actually participated. Instead, I would sit in the room with them while they felt the effects of whatever drugs they were on and would voice to me their experiences. I remember sitting back and laughing at them. I also remember my parents finding out that I had snuck out of the house during one period of grounding in order to go to my friends house and being grounded and punished for an even longer period of time. Being the rebel I was, I clearly was determined to not let anything curb my curiosity. Part of me regrets that, knowing the kind of strain that it eventually put on my relationship with my parents, as well as knowing that they'd never believe another word that came out of my mouth for the remainder of my life, based on the choices I made as a rebellious teenager. When things got far more serious in my life, they laughed at me and called me a liar yet again. But I digress.

By far I believe some of the most unusual friends I had in my youth were brothers, Steve and Don Shipley. For years I had an incurable crush on Steve, who was my age and grade. We had several classes together and I would tease him relentlessly. I was always boy-crazy, but my mother was convinced I would someday marry this crush. Steve and Don's mother was convinced equally that Don would one day marry his crush as well, except his crush just happened to be me. It made for many interesting stories involving the bus ride to and from school with the three of us being as close as we were. At the time, I wasn't being a very good role model, but I also didn't realize that Don looked up to me as much as he did. It wasn't until several years later that I realized a crush even existed.

I was a rather poor student at the time one particular adventure took place. Well, I wasn't exactly a bad student. I was actually quite a good student, when I was at school. I had started skipping classes, only a class or two at a time, the year before with Jimmy out of a sense of desperation and loneliness, and eventually it elevated to entire weeks the next year. That was about the time we drove out to Antelope Island, seven of us piled into a Volkswagen Rabbit. We even went so far as to ask two passengers to lay down in the trunk of the car so that they wouldn't be visible and it would appear that the car had a seatbelt for each passenger since the entry was manned by the highway patrol. I suppose I must have been about sixteen at the time, or almost that age. Not long after we got back from Antelope Island, I started spending a little more time with Steve's kid brother, Don. Don was most likely somewhere around the age of fourteen.

In the beginning, Don and I would just simply decide not to get on the bus in the mornings.

Lynn the bus driver would occasionally ask us about our absences, but we were rather vague. I'm sure it didn't look good to him. When one of us was absent, so was the other. Instead of getting on the bus, we would walk down to the park and meet at one particular place few other people knew about. From there we would decide on where to go and what to do. Sometimes we walked to the local western wear store and filled out job applications as though we were adults looking for full time work, knowing full well we wouldn't get hired for the job. Other days we would go browsing through the local music store or big box chain nearby. Occasionally we would be incredibly stupid and dodge the traffic on the freeway to get to the stores.. Nobody ever said anything to us about not being in school. Teachers didn't call, the principal never mentioned it to my parents. It seemed as though the school system in general didn't care if we showed up or not. Looking back, that seems to be one of the most suspicious events of the time. This was before the massive amount of school shootings we see these days, of course. It wasn't all that strange to the schools back then if the kids didn't show up, and it appeared like nobody cared about us. Eventually we were found out when our parents started to call the schools upon the discovery of report cards, but until then our secrets were safe, even as public as they were.

He and I had quite a few adventures, but none so memorable as the day we decided to stay at the park on a snowy, cold, frozen day and we tried to find some shelter. Don and I had explored the woods behind the old movie theater at the park many times in our adventures. We knew the trees and the paths through them almost as well as we would have known our own backyards at the time. It became our second home.

We headed up the winding open sewage creek towards the top of the hill, clambering and clawing our way up the muddy banks that were difficult on an average day and nearly impossible on a snowy or rainy day. Our feet slid through the mud leaving wide tracks as we scrambled our way up the muddy embankment past where the sewage pipe submerged from the sheer mud cliff. We emerged in a clearing and could see nothing around but trees. Nearby sat an old, wrecked, stripped, and rusted old mail van with the logos barely visible, just as lonely and abandoned as we were. About 50 yards away sat a tiny old wooden shack that we had never seen anyone go near. It reeked of history that we could smell through the winter air.

For a moment, we lingered in the old van, neither of us wanting to do what we both clearly knew was coming next, even without having to talk about it. By this point in our friendship, it was already clear to me that Don thought I was the toughest girl he had ever known, and had taken such liberty as to tell me so much on several occasions. For once in my teen life I had recognition. To one person, I stood out in a crowd. I was finally important to someone. I didn't want that to change in his eyes, or my own. To this day I'm not entirely sure if it was ego or pure stupidity that made me do what happened next, but one thing that will never change is that I did something I had thought I would never do. I broke some of the primary rules I set before myself that I swore I'd never break. My rule book was purely based in my brain, but I knew that they were my rules and my own basic principals. Perhaps I didn't have the greatest of friends or examples in my life growing up, but I had my core principles that I stood by. That is, until that day.

1. *Never do drugs.*
2. *Don't steal from anyone (except family)*
3. *Don't break what isn't mine.*
4. *Don't betray friendships.*
5. *Never hurt an animal.*

Don and I picked our way across the snow dusted field, being sure to only step on the tufts of grass on alternating sides all the way up the path. With each tip toe step on the protruding blades of grass we tried to leave footprints indistinguishable from the grass itself. We continued this way until we reached the old wooden shack. As we neared, we slowed even more, being even more deliberate with each step we took. Finally, we reached the old wooden surface of the building's outside, and I gingerly touched the gray, ancient planks. I knew from looking at it that the building had stood in that spot for at least the last 40 years, possibly more. One window looked into the building on the side where we stood, and not another window existed on the entire facade. That one window was of course too high and too dirty for little ones like us to see into. At the time I was barely five feet tall, and Don was several inches shorter than myself. We stood there a moment looking at one another. I pulled my brand new leather gloves I'd gotten for Christmas out of my pockets with frozen hands, and slipped my fingers into the leather extremities. My body heat had warmed the gloves as they snuggled deeply in my jacket pockets, and the warmth felt wonderful on my Popsicle fingertips. I clenched and unclenched my fist a couple of times in order to stretch the leather to my hand just so. I took a few deep breaths, concentrated mentally on what I was about to do, and finally held my breath. When I was ready, I struck. The sixteen inch high, one foot wide pane of glass shattered into a million pieces, sprinkling the ground inside with shards of all sizes.

Don stood back in awe. His mouth hung slightly ajar, his eyes wide with surprise. I opened my fist inside the window and with a flat palm, pulled more of the jagged hanging glass out through the fresh opening. I picked the broken glass out of the back of my now serrated brand new leather glove and tossed the glass into a nearby bush. In my heart I knew that what I had just done went against everything I had ever been taught and everything I myself had long since decided never to do, but at that moment, it just didn't matter to me. I wanted to hang on to that feeling of being important and being needed by someone in the world, even if the reasons behind it were completely wrong. I suppose at that moment that it was my ego getting the better of me. I wanted to remain someone who stood out in a crowd. I suppose that was the turning point. I've stood out nearly every day since. I've never broken into another building, but I've learned how to hang on to that feeling of being important. I also learned that I didn't need to do illegal things to have that feeling. All I really needed was to be able to help someone.

I dragged an unearthed tree stump from the nearby bushes and sludged it to the snow and muddy grass under the broken window. Once more I pulled the remaining loose glass from the window sill. Making sure my skin was properly covered everywhere first, I grabbed the rotten wood lining the window with a still gloved hand and shimmied into the opening up to my waist and looked around. I bent at the middle so I wouldn't require the strength of my arms to hold me up. I felt the edge of the window bite into my ribs and knew I hadn't been able to get all of the glass out of the way.   I took a breath and paused, reminding myself that I'd already come this far, there was no going back. The opening to the window was so small that I would have to turn sideways to get my hips through. I was much skinnier in my youth, and looking back on this incident, I know now that I wouldn't have been able to make this same move only a year later after my teen body began to develop more rapidly.

An old workbench lined the tiny wooden floored room to my left, it's edge nearly under the window and running the length of the left wall. Over to the opposite wall on the right and at the far end, an old glass-handled door remained closed. I couldn't imagine what treasures lay just beyond that door, just beyond what I could see. Even the room I was in was filled with treasures my brain was struggling to comprehend. Old rusted tools with fifty years of dust or more were scattered across the workbench. An antique tin tool box sat on the wooden floor under me, it's metal lid slightly warped to remain forever open, the curse of time leaving its mark upon the contents forever. Wooden handled screwdrivers lay still, covered in cobwebs and filth, the wood splintered and splitting from age and the elements. This was a child's paradise, a teenager's fantasy come true, and a history fanatic's paradise. It was the day that my love of history transpired from a love and into an obsession.

I tested the strength of the workbench with my left hand for stability and found it mostly trustworthy so I began to transition my body. I turned while resting on my ribcage, praying the glass wouldn't cut through to my torso though I could feel it scratching and grabbing at my clothing. When finally turned to a 90 degree angle to the ground I slowly pulled my twisted hips through the opening and struggled one leg to enter the window with the rest of me. I put one knee on the workbench as I pulled the other leg through the window. I felt like a gymnast performing for the circus, but felt like I somehow made it all look graceful. I have a feeling that it was anything but graceful at the time, however. I imagine I looked much like exactly what I was - an awkward teen trying to do something they shouldn't have been doing and feeling quite terrified at the time.

Once through the window, kneeling on the workbench, I felt better about my position. I patted myself to check for blood marks left by the glass before climbing down from the bench and landing on my feet. I turned to help Don climb inside then, paying close attention to everything around me. The wooden floor was elevated about a foot off the ground, so the window didn't seem nearly as high from my vantage point as it had from the ground outside. I peeked out and could still see the short boy's blond locks poking out in every direction under his dark blue knit cap. He elevated himself on his toes, and his blue eyes came into view.

"Step up on the wood," I whispered to him. His hands gingerly reached for the windowsill, cautious as he should be with no gloves on. I took a moment to pluck out the last few remaining shards of sharp glass to avoid him getting cut the way I feared I had done to myself.

"I'm already on it," he said with a bit of a sneer, thinking I was poking fun at his short stature. I couldn't help but smile to myself. He was terribly short, even for his age. Though it wasn't my intention to poke fun at that, it would have been an easy thing to do for almost anyone else. He reached through the window toward me and I grabbed onto his sleeves as he grabbed onto my own coat. I pulled on his arms as he braced his feet against the wall of the shack, trying to boost himself further than the tree stump would have otherwise allowed. Somehow he got turned around when his left foot slipped, and ended up looking at the ceiling with the rest of his body from his ribs down dangling out of the window like a rag doll.

"Eww! What's that," he asked, completely disgusted. I followed his gaze to the corner of the ceiling nearest the two of us. From a distance and in the naturally dark surroundings, they looked like little chicken drumsticks hanging on wire hooks from the ceiling. It seems like not only a weird thing to hang in a workshop or shed, but a rather gross thing to leave around anywhere until slightly molded and covered in cobwebs. I told Don not to worry about it, as was my usual answer, and pulled him the rest of the way inside. I was never an extremely graceful person myself, but Don's entrance made me look like a prima ballerina. He was all arms and legs, getting tangled crazily as he poured through the opening like a bundle of sticks attached by a single string. He landed on the floor in a pile and a groan.

As Don looked around, I became curious about the suspicious looking drumsticks he had spotted in the corner. I crawled cautiously onto the workbench on my knees, still not fully trusting the rotten wooden planks and pushing down with my hands to trust the stability before moving the weight of my body onto them. . They held my weight though, and I inched closer to the dangling random pieces.

I nearly screamed out loud. I bit my tongue to avoid shouting or letting any complaint escape my lips for fear of panicking my young companion. Those weren't just old chicken legs hanging in the corner. They were bats that had been tied upside down from wires around their feet so long ago that the flesh was rotting off the bones. Part of the skull was protruding in the area of each mouth, and the eyes were mere empty sockets of complete nightmare. They seemed to stare straight through me with complete nothingness. Just about the time I was going to jump down from the workbench and onto the floor, I saw one more hanging only inches above the window. It also happened to be only inches from my nose. The stench rolling off the rotted corpse gave away its location long before I saw it. I gulped and scrambled down from the table, not letting a syllable utter from my mouth. Don turned and looked at me.

"What's the matter with you," he asked. "You're white as a ghost. You feeling OK?" I didn't say anything for a moment, but I guess the way his expression changed as he watched me that he could see the wheels turning in my head. An evil grin slowly spread across my face.

"I got us in here," I began. "Now it's your turn." He looked puzzled at first. His eyes darted to the corner of the room and back to me again. Suddenly his face completely melted into an expression of pure fear.

"No way!" he cried out. His shout echoed off the snow covered ground outside.

Much to his immediate rejection at the thought, we searched around for something to help Don to get what he still thought were chicken legs out of the old shack. The two of us finally decided a pair of pliers and some old wire cutters would do the trick, so I grabbed an old keychain flashlight out of my pocket and got back up on the workbench. Don followed behind me, tools in hand.

Don clutched the base of the mystery object with the pliers toward the widest area of what he still thought was a chicken leg and something crunched under the pressure of his light grip. As if that wasn't bad enough, the decaying smell, something similar to that of road kill after it's been in the sun a few days, came wafting out, turning both our stomachs.

Don couldn't see the wire in order to cut it and our gagging increased. I knew that would be the case, though I really resisted using my flashlight as much as possible. Finally, I knew

I couldn't avoid it anymore. I tried to catch only the thin line of wire in it's beam, but the bony toes of the deceased bat were caught in the light beam. Don made lurching noises, and for a moment, I thought he was going to burst. He rocked back on his heels and I just barely caught him by the collar of his shirt before he fell off the table. Unfortunately, the light jarred in my hand when I reached for him and the dim illumination fell squarely on the now crushed head of the long dead bat. Something like oatmeal oozed out around the pliers. Every bit of color drained from Don's face, and I'm sure mine was a mirror image. Both of us lurched as though we were going to spew anything we'd eaten for the last several days. We stood there dry heaving for a moment trying to regain composure, knowing we needed to finish the task before we could do anything else. Neither of us would have been comfortable climbing out through the window so close to the dead bats, so we were trapped until we got the job done. We focused, regrouped, and encouraged one another to keep going. Of course that was much easier for me since it was deemed to be his task to get them out. My task was to make sure it was completed and to help as necessary. Fortunately I was the one who deemed if the assistance was necessary. According to my developed analytical mind, not much help was required from a second party as there was no heavy lifting involved and there was only enough room for one physical body at a time within close proximity.

Don flung the last of the dead mammals out the window as I stood back 'supervising' his giving the gift of flight back to the long dead bats, if only for a few seconds at a time.

THE SHACK

In The

WOODS

Part Two

THE SHACK

ON THE

INSIDE

Don and I met at the old shack nearly daily for a while that winter instead of at the bus stop. We'd have to meet outside and I would have to help Don in since he was too short, but it quickly became one of our favorite places to go on any given day. Occasionally when the snow was the heaviest, we would meet inside the old mail van nearby instead of the tree stump step stool.

We explored beyond the door the same day we got into the shack the first time, but not much. We knew that we'd made enough noise to possibly alert anyone nearby of our presence, and we needed to make sure the coast was still clear so we split pretty quickly that day. There was no point in risking the possibility of getting caught so early on. We needed to play it smart and be cautious. Getting out of the shack of course was much easier than getting in, but when we returned the next day and noticed that nothing looked different and the window hadn't been boarded up or barricaded, we knew that the sounds of our dry heaving didn't echo off of the snow outside as much as we might have feared.

It was finally time to explore the rest of the shack now that we knew we had it all to ourselves that following day. There still stood the mysterious wooden door with the glass doorknob at the end of that small room, on the far end of the workbench. The room beyond had once been a carriage house from the looks of it, long since used for storage. Dirt floors had been cluttered with various things, but faint wheel marks could still be seen from a history long past. A pedal powered knife-sharpening wheel sat by where the double doors once opened outward but had been sealed shut with wood as old as the rest, aged and weathered as though exposed to the elements for the last 50 years or more.

Antique brass headboards and footboards leaned against the wall at the back. Rusted spring-loaded animal traps hung from nails in the framework around each of the walls, all varying in size and shape. Ancient chains covered in grit and grime dangled next to machetes on the ceiling, held in place by nails and hooks alike. An old mule-pulled plow sat heavily on the ground next to the door inside. It was truly a treasure chest of ancient history to the eyes of a teenager.

I remember the first time I tried to use the stone grinding wheel to sharpen some of the old gardening tools we discovered in the shed. Being kids, we of course had lofty ideas about what we would do. I had it in my head that if I got the gardening tools prepared I'd be able to plant a garden come spring, with wildflowers and bean vines to crawl up the outside of the building. The grinding wheel was petal operated, but my feet and legs weren't strong enough to get the wheel going fast enough to actually sharpen the tools in my hand. I tried to turn the wheel with my hands to get it going, and while that did help, the old stone wheel was pitted enough that it would snatch the tools from my hand and fling them across the room.

A pile of glass doorknobs from the 1930s and 1940s sat in an old wooden milk crate. I would pick each one up gingerly and inspect it for cracks or chips. Each seemed to be completely pristine, and I marveled at the craftsmanship of each. They attached at the base of the knob to a brass fitting that had tarnished but was in otherwise perfect condition. The screws used to attach them to a door were still in place, still in the screw holes. There were a few locking brass door handles also that had the keys in a smaller wooden box at the bottom. The entire pile seemed to be completely forgotten by someone who didn't remember ever putting them out there in the first place.

Old wooden furniture, resembling a very tall dresser with very long legs, stood in the corner. The drawers were filled to the brim with what appeared to be old button down shirts and coveralls. They were far too big for Don or myself to even attempt to put on over our own clothes, and we had to venture a guess that the person who had owned this shed back when everything was placed so carefully within had been a farmer. The coveralls and old pull plow certainly spoke to a simpler time before big box stores, western wear culture, Goth style and anxious teens who felt like nobody cared about them. It spoke to a time when people lived with hard work and easy neighbors, with front porch friendships and lemonade while resting in the shade rocking in a rocking chair. It all seemed to come from a time long before our own; a time when our Grandparents might have spent their happiest days.

We went there many times over the coming months, and spring had started to thaw the ground beneath our feet eventually. The earth grew soft and the contents of the shed started to sink lower into the mud. Carefully, one at a time, with anything we were strong enough to lift, we would set on planks of wood or small boards in order to lift them out of the mess and back into the dry air where they would be safer. I knew that someday, someone would return to this shed and I'd hoped they would appreciate the history within as much as I had learned to. Until then, other than my grandmother's home, it was the oldest piece of tangible history I'd ever been in contact with. I wasn't willing to let it get ruined by a spring thaw. Of course it registered within my brain that it had been through many winters before I ever came around, but finally someone was paying attention and I wanted to preserve it as much as possible. It was a history worth saving, though it wasn't my own history.

Sometimes I think Don thought I was crazy for caring about a stranger's personal effects as much as I did, but I knew I had a duty to preserve what we could in spite of the fact that we had actually broken a part of it in order to find it in the first place. The glass that I'd broken, I discovered much later on, was actually lead glass with a warbled pattern to it. It wasn't smooth like the modern glass of today, but would warp the perspective of the person looking through the pane. Upon discovering how old that glass had been, my heart broke a little bit. I knew I'd destroyed a little piece of the history I held so dear to my own heart.

We started to hide things at the old shed. Of course I still stuck to my old personal rule of not doing drugs, so they weren't illegal things we would hide. We'd found a loose floorboard in the front room under the window and began storing small items under that as our secret hiding spot within our secret place. Don would hide a cassette tape he didn't want his brother to find or take away from him, and I would hide notes from my best gal pal at the time, the girl whose house I was staying at when the unfortunate incident occurred that required I end up receiving several stitches in my arm. We'd been forbidden to talk by my father. If he'd discovered the notes, he'd have been furious. We also hid other things there, like journals and diaries, money we would save up so we could have lunch together from time to time, incomplete homework that we didn't want family to locate, and more. I believe at one point in time I'd hidden a favorite pair of shoes in our space beneath the floor because they had gotten too small for me and my mother threatened to throw them out. Later on the hiding spot became crowded and I found other areas in which to hide our personal treasures among the treasures of who we deemed to be the forgotten farmer.

We made up stories about the Forgotten Farmer. We tried to imagine who he was, what his life must've been like and why all his personal belongings were eventually stored in the old shed as though they were to be forgotten along with him. We'd made up the name Richard for this man, and Richard had been a kind person with a good heart. He had a wife and five children who helped him to keep up with the farming on his property before eventually selling most of it off to the movie theater company. When the theater was built Richard's heart broke because it meant that he wouldn't be able to grow his own corn and wheat anymore. He had to downsize his farm to a large garden, and while he sold off most of his cattle he kept one Guernsey cow for fresh milk and companionship, as Betsy has always been a good cow to him. Eventually Richard grew old, as did his land and his family. His wife Margaret was a sweet lady who looked a lot like Mrs. Claus with her spectacles on the end of her nose and she always smelled like moth balls and vanilla, a scent I was familiar with for my own grandmother smelling much that way. She was portly and kind with apple cheeks and a white apron she wiped her hands on constantly out of habit. She loved baking pies and cookies, and before Richard passed away she would bring his lunch out to the old shed where he would be tinkering with the animal traps and tools, fixing some little tidbit of something that had broken in their aging home. His kids had all grown up and moved away many years before.

By the time Richard passed away, in our imaginations, his wife had gone a few years before him. He hung around because of his grandkids, and he wanted to see hif first great grandchild. When finally his oldest grandson was old enough to take a wife and eventually have a child, they decided to name their newborn son after Richard himself. With that, Richard's greatest life achievement was finally fulfilled, and he passed away peacefully in his sleep. He willed the shed and all of the land to that same great grandchild, to be cared for by his parents until he was old enough to take over what was left of the property himself. Of course, it had been so many years at that point since the shed had been used regularly that nobody really remembered that it was out there. As they cleared out the old house in order to do renovations, much of Richard's leftover stuff ended up being tucked into the shed. The box full of doorknobs came from the renovation, as did the old highboy dresser where Richard kept most of his farming clothes. Eventually the weeds grew up and the family forgot that the shed ever existed at all. We imagined that Richard's family didn't forget about him, for surely there were photos of him in the old house, all with the torn edges of ancient photographs, all in black and white. We pictured him in the coveralls we found, and a button down plaid printed shirt, his arm around his lovely wife, standing beside their first brand new car, a 1932 Packard. In the arms of Margaret was a brand new baby, the first of five.

What vivid imaginations we had as children. I often think back on those days and wonder if a person like Richard ever existed, and if he did, how many children he ever had. I know now that the mystery of the shed will never be solved, but in my mind back then we knew all of the history. There was nothing on the planet that could convince us otherwise. We had the entire story made up between the two of us.

We kept that shed our little secret for a few years. We would meet there before school sometimes, and occasionally we would go there afterward. Summers were often spent in our quiet little place, telling stories to one another. Don grew up and got older, though he didn't get much taller. His brother spouted several inches one summer and I clearly remember Don being incredibly upset that none of the height was passed on to himself. All the time we continually played at the shack in the woods, we never shared our secret with anyone. That's not an easy thing for a kid to do, of course. But we knew it was worth it. It needed to be our secret. If a secret like that got out, not only would others invade the private place, but it would be discovered that kids had been playing inside and it would eventually be taken away from us completely. If we were going to keep it a secret, we couldn't share it with anyone other than one another.

I had aspirations back then of someday being an actress. I never would have thought myself to be pretty enough to pull it off, but the bug bit quite early on. A kid in class wrote a play when I was in the 6th grade and, no matter how terrible an actor she was, she got the lead role. From then on I started writing my own plays and acting out every role in an effort to better myself. When I auditioned for the school play as a kid I was given the nondescript task of walking across the stage holding a large fake clock to show the passing of time. I wasn't pretty enough or talented enough to get any other role and it broke my heart and spirit for a while. Now, here I was with my own breathing wooden time capsule and all the materials I could ever imagine wanting to need for my own historical dramatic play at my disposal. I can't count the hours I would spend in that shack, acting out some routine or scene in the most over the top dramatic way I could, just as any sixteen-year-old kid would do. We were eventually able to find ways to stealthily move some of the furniture around within the confines of the space without making a lot of grunting sounds so as to leave any passersby in the dark about our intentions or actions. Toward the back, behind the highboy dresser, had been hidden a smaller makeup table with an ancient, cracked, brass backed beautiful oval mirror, likely from the 1930s art deco period in American History. I would open the drawers with such caution and care that it seemed as though I were rocking a baby in the bough of a tree. It was in front of this mirror where I began to practice some of my favorite monologues from movies.

It was around that time that my parents decided to begin taking away all of my personal belongings. Everything began to disappear, from my bedframe and music to my clothing and bedroom door. With everything I owned slowly vanishing I needed to find a way to hide what I had left. The shack came in handy yet again. I began to use the empty space in the highboy and makeup table to stash my own private items. I hid my contraband makeup, which I wasn't supposed to even own, in the delicate art deco drawers, and my clothes in with the coveralls. Sometimes I would have a favorite dress that I knew would be taken away if it were so much as seen off of my body, so that was a quickly hidden garment. Eventually I started hiding other things, too. Teddy bears, gifts from friends, candles my parents were convinced would burn down the house if entrusted to my hands... they all got stashed in the shack.

It started to feel more like home than the place where I lived with my parents. At least in the shack I wasn't called a liar, threatened with more possessions being taken away from me, and treated as a house slave, only allowed to clean or do homework.

I began to break more of my own rules then. As much as I didn't want to walk that road, I began to steal. I didn't blatantly steal things for the thrill or to make money off of them, but for necessity. Eventually my parents believed the only items I had left were one change of clothes and a nightgown I would change into a nightgown in order to wash my day clothes. Everything else, with exception of the sheets on a mattress that rested upon the floor, was gone. There were no books, but no bookshelf for them to sit upon anyway. There were no pencils to draw with, but no paper to draw upon. There were no musical instruments but no music to read or play. There were no toys, no dolls, no friends. My room was as barren as the Sahara in the summer, aside from the mattress. That was when I began to steal.

The kids at school began to tease me and ask

me daily if I'd worn the same clothes to school the day before. I started getting called "smelly" and was accused of being homeless. Beyond mortified, I did what I felt was my only course of action as a teen with no income, but a backbone of steel and a sense of purpose. I went to Goodwill.

I started with a single pair of jeans. They were easy enough to get out of the store. I would go into the changing room and put the jeans on over top of my own, and I was so thin at the time I looked medically fragile. Then I would put a shirt on under the oversized shirt I was wearing. From there, I would exit the Goodwill store as though that was how I walked in, and nobody was any the wiser. The people at Goodwill never questioned me, though I went in at least once a week for a while, and never walked out wearing exactly what I walked in with. Everything that I stole from Goodwill went to the shack, knowing full well that if it was ever discovered I would be punished severely and accused of far worse. That was the usual way in our household. They all got sequestered into the drawers of the dresser and makeup table, hidden well from sight and prying eyes. To this day I have a problem with hoarding personal items based on the psychological damage done to me in my teen years, where I felt anything would be taken away from me at any moment simply because someone bigger or stronger or of more authority says it should be. I don't let go of things that no longer fit me. I will only discard items after I know I haven't worn them for at least three years or more. And when I do get rid of them, they go straight to Goodwill. I will never be able to repay the kindness I received from them simply by never saying a word when I had to steal my clothes to avoid being beat up at school. I'll never forget how precious it was to have that shack when I needed it most, in order to hide all of my treasures that seemed to give me a glimmer of hope when everything else in my life seemed to be caving in on me. Truly, I was desperate. I still haven't forgiven myself for stealing, but I've never stopped long enough to question how much I needed that precious old shack in the woods at the time. My life was in turmoil, and there wasn't a single place on earth that offered me peace and safety other than the place that belonged to a person I never met. I'd lost everything, as far as they knew, except my spirit. That shack hid more than just my contraband clothing and forbidden makeup. It hid where my spirit rested. It concealed more than just material possessions. It concealed my inability to give up on having some corner of my own in the world where I couldn't be tortured and nobody would take what I had away. I spent some of the best and worst days of my life out there at the shack. I never did the things I was accused of, like doing drugs or having sex, but I certainly hid from the world the person I was learning to become.

I did go through drug withdrawals in that shack. It was the legal kind - I'd been put on ritalin when I was only 4 years old and decided when I was fifteen that I needed to take myself off of the pills. It threw my body into a massive withdrawal after eleven years of a highly controlled substance. I became depressed and withdrawn, preferring to wear all black clothing and contemplating the end of life more than once. If I were ever going to do it, that would have been the place to make the world disappear forever. I had the means, but I didn't have the desire. Looking back now I know that as much as I wanted the pain to end, and as much as I wanted everything else to go away, I also didn't want to die. I needed things to end, but not like that. So I kept on living in spite of what I had been going through. The shack kept on drawing me back. I'd sit there in silence sometimes for hours, simply thinking to myself and wondering what would happen to the lives around me if I did end up dying out there. Don would have been the only person on earth who would've known where to look for me, and even he knew I was going through far too much. He knew it wouldn't do any good to come find me, so most days he just let me be alone. He knew I needed my space and that nothing could drag me away from the recesses of my own mind right then. I was clearly going through something, and if sitting at the old workbench and tinkering with wooden handled tools doing basically nothing but trying to learn how they worked was helping me, that's exactly what he would let me do.

One day I tried to move the old mule plow on my own while Don was at school. I couldn't get it to budge no matter how hard I pushed and pulled. I finally laughed at myself, having to admit that I wasn't as strong as a mule, only as bull headed and stubborn as one would expect a mule to be. But, being that bull headed, of course I wasn't willing to give up. I tried again and again, eventually even using some old rope that I'd found in the shack to tie onto the handles and attempt to drag it from the ground it had been sunk into for many years. I pulled until the ropes bit into my hand leaving small splinters all through my palm, fibers embedded into my skin. Still I pulled. I wrapped the rope over my shoulder against my neck and turned my back on the plow and tried again, leaning forward with all my might. The rope again bit into me, this time leaving its deeply embedded burn in my neck where it made contact. Finally I gave up on moving the old plow and it remained exactly where we'd found it. Eventually I turned it into a seat by stacking a board over the sharp surface and covering it with an old blanket. The handles became the spine of my homemade chair and I spent more hours than I care to contemplate resting there quite comfortably. That night I was accused of having sex with strangers, and the rope burns surely must have been hickies.

A canoe hung from the low hanging rafters of

the shack. For a while I had no idea what to
do with it other than to leave it where it was,
and perhaps hide things within it. Eventually
I decided that I wanted to do something more
with it. We'd used canoes quite often when I
was a kid. Our family would take canoe trips
back when we were still happy, back before
the family dynamic changed forever. I worked
for days to clear a space in the floor so that I
could bring down the canoe and inspect it
closer. It was being held up by nothing but an
old rusted chain and a couple of electrical
cords tying it to the beams above. Crooked
nails were bent on purpose to give the cords a
place to grip onto. When finally I was able to
have a space for the canoe, I got a pair of old
pliers from the workbench area and went to
work. They weren't wire cutters, so the effort
was long and difficult, and took several days
to accomplish, but I went to work. I reached
high over my head and pinched the electrical
cord with the pliers and began to twist round
and round in circles, never losing my grip on
the pliers or the cord, spinning until the canoe
was taught against the rooftop with no slack
in the electrical cable. The cord began to
crush the hull of the wooden canoe then, so I
had to unwind the cable and begin to twist in

the opposite direction. Days and weeks were spent in this position, my arms cramping over my head and my dizzy spells increasing as I spun in circles until I was ready to vomit. Eventually the cord would be completely taught the other direction and I'd have to start back again the other way once more. After several days the cord was finally weak enough that it began to fray.   I increased my concentration, and one day in the middle of my twist the canoe finally popped loose and cracked me in the skull. I don't remember much for several moments. I woke up laying flat out on the mud floor, my head pounding viciously.   I had been knocked unconscious. Nearby the canoe dangled from the ceiling on one end, the other end neatly buried in the mud. There was a chill in the air and I knew night had settled in while I lay there unconscious. That night when I got home, I was accused of having been hiding at some boys house, obviously having sex.

The frame of an old cot sat in the corner. It looked like it had been made of wood almost 200 years ago, but surely wasn't quite that old. The mesh was torn and frayed, and somehow I imagined that it had been used during WWII by old Richard himself. A few times during the deepest turmoil at home I toyed with the idea of running away and staying at the shack. I never did, but only because I knew there was no food available if I did that. I'd rather be able to eat and go through psycological torture than to go hungry and torture myself physically. I would sometimes lay on that cot and just stare at the ceiling for hours, trying to have 'happy thoughts' the way I was taught as a four year old child in my attempts to chase the nightmares away. I suffered from terrible nightmares in my youth. To some degree, they still plague me. During the days when I had that peaceful place in the shack, the nightmares weren't so bad. I learned how to deal with my own demons a little at a time. The nightmares were never as bad then as the thoughts that crossed my mind while I was awake. I suppose my dreams figured I was being tortured enough in real life, there was no work left to do against me.

THE SHACK

In The

WOODS

Part Three

THE SHACK

We Left

BEHIND

Winter was setting in once again. After my brain finally started to calm and I found myself to be in much less turmoil, though still very much going through everything that I'd come to know as my daily life, Don started coming around again. I seemed less angry, though still very determined and bull headed. I'd even run away for a while, going off to Arizona with a few other runaways. Still very much the troubled teen that I always had been, I had begun to figure out who I was on the inside. The drug withdrawals were gone, my parents stopped trying to force me to see a therapist who viciously tried to force me into admitting to all the sex I wasn't having. I think my parents had finally discovered that they would not be able to break my spirit as they had hoped.   If anything, it had strengthened tremendously.

I knew Don was as tired as I was of climbing through the tiny window opening after the amount of time we'd spent over the passing years, if not more so. Clearly I spent more time at the shack than Dan ever had, but My mind, ever-devious back then, came up with a plan one day.

"Hey Don, why don't you check out the side doors from the outside, see what they're locked with. Maybe we can find a key and use that as our door from now on," I explained after telling him that I'd discovered an old wooden box full of keys under a floorboard in the small room. Delighted at the idea, he hurried out the window as fast as his round, short body would allow, and ran around the building to the other side of the doors. After explaining to me what the lock looked like, I began to make guesses as to which key would be the right one. I slid the keys one by one under the door, and one by one Don tried them all and passed them back.

"I got an idea," Don said to me, after the last key was safely back in its box. I heard him run back around the building and I met him at the window in the next room "Hand me that saw," he said, pointing to the workbench. I handed him the wood saw, not knowing exactly what he was going to do with it, and went back to the inside of the double doors as he tossed his jacket inside along the wall.

First, Don tried to saw a bracing board in two with the rusted blade, and when that didn't work, decided to try the metal chain and lock that held it in place. Finally fed up with the resistance, Don grabbed a rock, determined to smash the lock apart. All the noise he was making should have raised the dead bats from their shallow two year old grave. Just about the time I was going to tell him to stop, to be quiet, I heard a strange voice.

"Hey Kid," a deep, growling voice yelled. "Get away from there!" Heavy footsteps outside warned me that whoever it was decided walking wasn't getting them to Don quite fast enough. I heard Don's rock drop to the ground and I knew he was gone, running like a mad man through the woods. I was trapped inside.

There were apparently two men who had come to investigate. I could overhear them talking as they made their way around the inspection of the shed. I crawled, silent as a mouse, into the smaller room and hid under the corner of the work bench closest to the window.

"Aw, shit. Look at this, Chuck," the one who had yelled at Don said. I didn't need to look in order to know what he was talking about. The man was standing right over me, looking in through the window. I held my breath. "That damn kid broke the window." They couldn't have known it had been that way for two years and counting.

"I s'pose we should nail it up before it snows tonight," the other replied. "Let's get a board and some nails." I heard the two start walking back the way they came and my spirits lifted. They were just about back to the double doors when I heard them pause.

"Wait," the one named Chuck paused. "What if the brat comes back?" he asked. "I better wait here while you get the stuff."

My body sprang into action before my mind had time to think. I jumped up, my head glancing off the table above me, and stood before the window. I knew without a doubt that they heard my head hit, and I didn't have much time.

I leapt into the air and twisted my body miraculously like an Olympic diver would off a high dive and instead of diving into water, I sailed through the open window. Just before passing all the way through, I saw Don's only winter jacket on the floor by the wall where he had left it. It was too late. I could only pray he didn't have any identification in it. Briefly I thought of all my own belongings I would be leaving behind and my heart sank. I wouldn't miss the spare jeans and warmer winter shirts as much as I would the art deco makeup table with the cracked oval mirror.

I landed on my hands and rolled roughly onto my back, catching a sharp stone right in the kidney. An old branch tore at my leg and tore my jeans. I heard shouting behind me and didn't take the time to catch my breath after the landing knocked it out of me. I pulled my feet under my sore butt and fled down through the woods, I imagine much the same way Don had run.

It wasn't long before I caught up to Don and passed him. My legs were much longer.

Neither of us skipped a single class in school for a month. Eventually Don's mother began asking where his jacket had gone. Not knowing what else to tell her, finally he just said that I had it and would get it for him. The retrieval of his jacket was the last time I ever went back up that hill in the woods, but that's another story.

THE END

Other Books

Written By

Amanda Blackwood

Non Fiction

- The Miller Miles
- Detailed Pieces of a Shattered Dream
- Thirty Synchronized Woodpeckers
- Twisted Fate
- Custom Justice
- Lost April

Science Fiction

- The Unlikely
- New Hope
- Fair Play